# SAD GIRL STRONG WOMAN

## A Poetry Book

by

Alyssa N. Griego

www.alyssangriego.com
ISBN:987-0-692-07459-6
Edited by Antonio Campos
Cover/interior design by Lena Pozdnyakova
Printed in the United States of America.

For the ones
they left behind

L.M.

Logline: A young Chicana writer pursues a lustful troubled woman, Rain, embarking on a two year spiritual journey of love, creation, betrayal, and acceptance.

P.S. My skin reeks of the childish girl I used to be, and the guerrilla warrior I've become. I am nothing less than resilience, and that can never be fiction...

# Contents

# DESIRE

<u>MAY 5, 2015</u>

         I stare at your pictures
       As if you are the beginning
          And end of me...

-First Good Morning

Good morning

I don't know your name
Or the reasons why you came,
But this is a morning saying

There may be truths behind
your eyes
There may be beauty in
disguise

Shoot I may never know
Or I may hear the heartbeat
slow,
Snaps it snaps
The Jazz is playing
Like sun rays on Sundays
Making you crack a smile,
With a cracked lip
I'll speak on it.

Head to the park
Watch the kids blossom,
Or you could tell me to kick
rocks
Then the ink blots
Would be crumbled and tossed
out the window,
The chips of paint aren't
that simple.

I can't sing like John
Legend
I can't rap like Blu
But I can wrap you up
With good mornings,
Good afternoons,
Hips too.

Do you prefer your coffee
black or with cream?

<u>MAY 23, 2015</u>

-She Asked Me What Happiness
Was

She asked what happiness
was,
I pointed to a dream journal
Told her to write the curves
to her soul
So purple, sow virtue.

The missing puzzle pieces
she could never let go,
The raindrops from the
willow trees
That poured slow,
When her lover,
Could not hear her heartbeat
anymore.

She sat there staring at me
Pondering, what to squeeze
out of her plump lips---
The sound of her eyes
penetrated
My glasshouse,
But I did not kiss her
I did not touch her
I just read the words tucked
in her skin
The records skipped, once
again.

And I can tell
The unspoken words were the
watermelon
Sounds I could never taste.
Let the fingertips create
another language
That drips whispers
None can decode.
The music never grew cold.

It was the happiness growing
from her lips
That she didn't notice
I think there's the pursuit
of happiness on her lips,
But she was so soft-spoken
She didn't know this.
I opened the dream journal,
And there she was.
Sublime colors she was---
A concrete flower, yes she was.

<u>MAY 27, 2015</u>

- Dear Diary

Air, barely breathing
Air it's steaming

Bare, emotions reaching.
Volcano peaks, walks with a
couple drinks.

You're trying to figure out
what I contemplate
It doesn't matter,
Built these lines from paste
and brick,
I can feel your energy
It's telling me,
You want to rock with me.
Adding light, to these flames
igniting
Shape shifting
You can be the moon lady
Blue moon, body language
I can tell you never fell,
I could assume, but I rather
you show me
Sigh--- language, get to
know my body.

Brown love
Wishing wells
Only time can tell
And I can't tell the time,
Throwing pennies and dimes
For a dime like you
Self-sacrificing, if it's
just us two
Aztecs, trees, souls,
Thank you
For cultivating a woman with
an ocean breeze
Either way I'm drifting

You're a wonder woman.

S on the chest, sex face
Sexy.
Catch those waves, relax
arched backs
Saving memories, to
celebrate or create collages
Montages.
Directing on these---
While our lips meet and
greet
Let my palms pave

I know it's depth that you
crave
Parachuting until we cave.

15

Round two, curves and
mountains
Ain't no pyramid high enough

I'm high, but not enough
To stop monasteries and
caress your lips
There are flowers growing
from it
I can taste your soul---
mate.
Checkmate, it.

Blurry vision captivating
me,
Could you be my twin flame?

Savoring your mango soul
You call me a queen,
I'm the knowledge
In your favorite scene.
This is seamlessly
impossible,
All my life they told me
A love this rich was
dispensable.
We are breaking family
cycles,
My eyes fill with tears
When you look at me
If this isn't love

I don't want to be,
This close to she.
Down south, it's an acquired
taste,
I want to build an empire
upon your waist
Up, up with God's grace
Angel face.
There are angels all around
us
Wake up next to me
Wrestle dawn and sheets
Pickpocket my mind
And you can have it all.

- I Want To Kiss You

You are music, putting me in a trance
As my body lies there, my spirit rises

                    High  enough, to a point
                where I am not high enough
                Not to remember, but to savor
        the moment where my mind surrenders.

Outside my body, I can see us.
As our lips become roses, I think my
soul was fed water
Swaying to the beat, until it grew feet.

                        Then I met the sky,
                Your eyes became the moon
                    And I died every time
                    Just to see you rise

Your sunshine is so bright,
As the sun kisses mine.
My universe touched yours
And as I open my eyes,
I was reminded what happiness, felt like

                So radiant, we can be so radiant
                    That your fingers walked in
                        And wrote a chapter on
                                    my skin.

My soul surrendered,
I secretly think the barriers
Of my bones collapsed

       We traveled to another galaxy
         That's what it feels like,
      When your tongue speaks to me
      Creating a language in the sky

Just like our peoples
We teach each other how to evolve
And die.
     I am the moon and you are the sun
       You rise over the Great Wall
         And I fall into the
           underworld

Battling off my demons, so you and I can
keep dreaming.
Then I rise and you fall, as you are
screaming
There's ecstasy and pain

     But every kiss makes us tear down
          Our walls
     And the mud and brick, repair our
          muscles
       Only to feel stronger.

I think it makes the beat stronger
I think I am scared,
Of your power

I am scared that feelings might heighten
                    I think I, I think I
                  Want to know how you
                                feel?

These moments,
Taste like fire and ice.
                        Both perishing
                  Until I meet you,
                  Until I see you.

<u>JUNE 24, 2015</u>

My sky
Is trapped in your eyes
Brown, not blue
Passion fruit,
Licking all of you
Accept yourself---
We are not whiteness.

<u>JUNE 25, 2015</u>

I glanced at she
She glanced at me
She pictured three
My palms felt a we

I think she fell for me

A future isn't unheard of,
But with globalization it's
hard to achieve

She is deciding if the devil
is more bound to my ankles,
Like two clenched fists
All fingers point to herself.
When all roads lead to
yourself
It's difficult to smash the
brick,
Never letting anyone in.

If my thoughts become words
on some paper they do crave,
You were my first love

You conjure up spells
That make my heart move from
cold to hot
Boiling point---
You are the Solar System.
Mom would be proud
Our eyes speak loud---

Our spirits rolled in the
clouds

I glanced at she
She glanced at me
She pictured three

I think I have fallen for
her...

- Your Body Is My Home

I thought I didn't have a
home
So I searched through
crowds.
I didn't have a home---
So I passed through girls
and boys.

Never knowing what home felt
like
Never knowing if the rhythm
of the bass would hold me
Infiltrating my essence

I stopped and your long wavy
hair kissed my cheeks
Your fingers trickled down my
lips
And at that very second I
touched your skin
I died a little bit.

To only be reborn,
I've been home ever since
The gates clip the bottom of
my heels
Then the light danced in my
limbs

Only to make my knees lose
all control
My body tumbled into you.

And you,
You hold me
And I am free.

For the first time
My wings can breathe,
They flap and now you see
You and I
Eye to eye.

It takes a lot to get close
to me,
Yet you are holding more
than just my body.

Move, move
Close, closer
Come back home to me.

<u>JULY, 2015</u>

It takes thirst to
understand the drought

Takes experience to
understand what they are
talking about

Never remaining static,
except when staring at you

Collecting colorful images
of what they cannot see

If this is just a dream,
will you remember me?

You are Diego
And I am Frida
I want to crack you open
Spilling the rush on my
sheets,
Drinking your chocolate
Again and again

- Demand my love, forever.

# UNCERTAINTY

Why do you believe you
deserve love,

When your family is a
wasteland...

I am

Darkness and illumination

Mixed in one.

I never needed two---
Or three?

I just thirst for you,
Or me?

Like a cup of lavender tea---
Or café?

I enjoy you every morning
after,

Our simmering nights.

I wedge myself

    Between happiness and
uncertainty

      Forcing myself to eat

        Now and never

- When You Go Missing


If you have power in your
left palm,
Someone's heart in your
right
Would you combine the two

Or continue to write your
poetry?

Hope they don't notice me.

Just let the earphones lose
it.

Your memory haunted our
people,
In our dreams, dreams
embedded
With bloody knuckles and
moans

The honesty is growing in
the genes

You say your love hurts, you
love to hurt

You love so much, you don't
even know your worth.

Feel the iron on your chest,
it's heavy
Take my thought and soul---
are you ready?
Letting one talk to you like
that

Is as belittling as
fences---

You are not white, you are
not brown
They treat you like you have
no heart
Rip it out and point it to
the sky,
Sacrifice your feelings for
what's right.

How life would be,
If I continued with poetry
How life would be,
If I would walk away from
those that hurt me
How life would be,
If I took a step toward them
arguing.

Wondering, as I step into my
reflection

If there is a savior within
me
Willing to save me.

From the turmoil I have
learned to ignore
From the demons that devour
the core,
Issues.

Aches pulse through my arms

And my wrist snaps--- pops

It's torn ligaments,
It's my cousins' busted lip
It's my mom's fucked-up
teeth

From my sister's

Daddy's grief.

I would stand up, but I
stand down for it
You love, you, you, love
You love hurt, you love to
hurt

Love so much, don't know
your worth

Love, lover
Love me better
If you love someone else
Better you,
Than us together.

I am not a pocketbook,
Or a poet who needs new
lines.
There's blood in your nails
Your teeth shine

Love, I love so hard
I love this far
I feel their heart
I feel the scabbed skin
From their sin.

You love so much, you love
enough for the both of them
You waste enough, that
there's nothing left for
you.

Oh, lover
I wonder how you breathe, in
and out
How you breathe, in and out
When there is,
Just violence, words, and
shouts.

When there is,
Just violence, words, and
shouts.

- Friends

You apologize for your
friend,
As if you have done this
before

And I,
Always believe all that you
say,
Because,
It is you.

INT. COFFEE SHOP - DAY

ALYSSA (20) and the exquisitely
beautiful designer RAIN (22) calmly sit,
wedging themselves between a wooden
table.

Rain slowly takes a sip. Carefully,
admiring Alyssa.

                    RAIN
              You're gonna be an
              amazing person.

Uncertain, Alyssa responds.

                    ALYSSA
              Going to be?

Confidently leaning toward Alyssa.

                    RAIN
              You are. But if we
              don't work out
              and in two years you're
              single and I'm
              single. Hit me up.

Her heart sinks. She forces a smile, as
Rain softly kisses her hand.

                    ALYSSA (V.O.)
          You say goodbye, as if
          you are God,
          and I always, say
          hello.

L O S T

### AUGUST 2, 2015

I embrace her in this summer
dew,

Telling her I wouldn't be
the same

When I return. This
addiction has become
unbearable.

Could our bodies last one
month apart

As I search for my face,

In unpredictable places, in
Mexico.

### AUGUST 4, 2015

(Oaxaca, Mexico)

I sent her a message, yet
she didn't respond.

I am lost, again in another
country,

When I thought she, was my
only home.

- Raining In Oaxaca

Come paint with me,
Paint me please

My eyes are red,
My hands are yellow,
My skies are blue
Rain keeps pouring in Oaxaca
for you.

I gave her all of me
Without knowing if she
wanted all of me

It is embodied in the
thunder

This will be the death of me
I think she wants to be free
Though I had a love so
vibrant

Starving, gasping, paint
smashing
As the memories collide.

Can you feel me?
Can you hear me?

Am I painting on my own?

Tell me, before the oxygen
disappears
Get the paintbrush make it
clear.

Smear my mascara, paint my
eyes
So beautiful as I embrace
her lies.

She doesn't understand how I
feel,
Because I feel everything.

Now you are running from me,
Fast, faster pony

There she goes, and I,
Watch her.
I always watch them leave
With the morning sun

Pinks and blues

Paint it black, my soul too

Cut my heart out
And give it to the Gods.

I searched for fruit in your
eyes,

But I only found death
  In their stomachs,
    In my chest,
    In my chest.

- Raw Almonds // And You Nothing

One day they will recall
How they treated me

Only to recall the brew,
Falling into theirs

Just like every other woman
You too have plucked all my petals
Leaving me to rot

Never realizing how strong
The stem was,
Never watching it--- it grew

Despite the words, despite the lies
I can smell the scent of raw almonds.
It is coming from their breath

Oh, one day they will recollect
That flower
Only to regret, not adding water.

They will fall into theirs
Because a flower with bruises is
beautiful.

The almonds taste bitter,
The almonds they forced are bitter.

INT. A LOFT - DAY OAXACA, MEXICO

Exhausted. Depleted. Alyssa and her
research partner MARIPOSA (22) lug their
suitcases into the loft of a stylish
painter JUAN (52).

Juan swiftly pours them all wine,
quickly speaking in Spanish. She tries
to decipher what he says. We hear WHITE
NOISE. Losing focus, Alyssa glances at
her phone. TEXT reads from Rain I CAN'T
DO THIS ANYMORE.

Her phone slips from her hand. Thoughts
are racing. Sick. She slowly looks up.
Strangers are smiling at her in all
directions. Alyssa suddenly excuses
herself to the bathroom.

Pushing her body through the door.
Everything is spinning, violently.
Desperately gripping her head. She
squeezes her eyes. Her eyes are
waterfalls. She dials her mother's
number.

She HEARS her mom scream in the
background. A FRIEND answers.

                    FRIEND (O.S.)
          Get her out of the room!
          Okay, Alyssa.
          Are you okay? Hmm, your
          grandpa just passed away.
          We're gonna get you home.

She bursts into tears. Silently forcing
her fist in her mouth, she quiets her
sobs. Forcing herself to breathe, she
shakes her head as if it will take her
back in time.

                    ALYSSA
          Just. Hmm, called. You
          know. That girl. Hmm

Losing all sense. She hangs up.

Trying to coach herself out of her
shock, she stares into the mirror.
Shutting her eyes.

                    ALYSSA (V.O.)
          It's okay. I'm fine. I
          got this. I'll just tell
          them. I'll go to bed.


Clearing her mascara. She inhales.
Grabbing her cap. She covers her bloodshot eyes. Slowly exiting.

## AUGUST 19, 2015

In the end they will leave
So here's a note to myself
Just let them leave
Turn the leaves
Take a breath, and breathe

It doesn't matter
I don't matter

Nothing matters
Words don't matter
There is no grey matter
Dark matter,
Pussy matter

I do not matter
I cannot matter

I thought I knew it all
Until I realized,
I didn't know anything at
all
Until I hit the ground and
fall
I cannot matter

It is just ashes in a memory
That's all we'll ever be

Dirt in the floor
Blisters to sores

You can give your all
And they will always take
Giving nothing in return
To return you, back to the
floor

Back to the floor
Back to the floor

Dirt, dirt, more,
More.

<u>AUGUST 21, 2015</u>

We sent text messages as if
we're playing chest,

Relishing the strings to my
chest

As I stare at the coffin

Continuously, mourning my
grandfather's death.

<u>AUGUST 27, 2015</u>

Pouring bottle after bottle
I drown you from my heart,
Until I can only spot
darkness.

- Happy Birthday Alyssa

I cannot give you much right
now
But I have given you my
words,
My last breath, the aches
between my breasts

I cannot give you much right
now
But I have made you into a
Goddess
Painting stories with my
adjectives.

Who else would take the
time,
When there isn't much time
To conjure up stories, to
tell you
I love you, when my own soul
Has become empty and numb

I cannot give you much,
But I have given more than
The woman you will date,
More than the woman you will
marry.

And in my mind,
I have given you a seed,
I have given you my air to
breathe,

I have given you my baby,
And you have taken all

Strengthening and wiggling
the deep cracks
In my heart like a loose
tooth
Filling them with
silhouettes and unkempt
promises

I cannot give you much right
now,
But you have taken too much
So I lost myself,
And momentarily fell

I cannot, I cannot
You have not, you have not
earned this.

## SEPTEMBER 19, 2015

Found my faith on the corner
of a street
Where drugs meet and greet
Where women get beat,
My heart beats, it doesn't
stop
And I heard a rumor---
Down on Second Street,

Looking up I asked for a
sign
Their verbiage speaks
Raging violence of five
hundred years
On these sheets,

Now my skin tastes dry and
raw
Like the lies that crawl and
stomach aches
That kiss bathroom stalls

I heard a rumor,
But it was nothing at all.
Just a truth folded in your
pocket
Described as a beauty, yet I
seen
The ugly as you spread my
chest
It's nothingness

Depressed, as she tied
Her ropes of words around my
wrists
Then my ankles
I looked up blood fell
And I wept

Only to spot
A woman with a halo
Looking down on me.
She was there all along,
But I was too blind to see
Plastic cups and sin
diminished my vision

I heard a rumor, but it was
true
Beauty lies within
The breakdown.

EMPTINESS

I take her back
Knowing she will never
stay...

-September 22nd

## SEPTEMBER 28, 2015

Set me free,
From the burdens of
disillusion
Salt pours through my vision
Deep down I love all of she
Whether that includes or
excludes me

Another day, another liqueur
Another day to die quicker

They are picking me apart,
Like I? Am--- invincible...
What do I have to do,
To be visible
To be love-making syllables

I am only human.

I am incapable of being
complacent

Cherish this love or replace
it.

- N(ice) Dreams

Think we found something
more than pain and suicide

But love brings pain, then
suicide

For a girl of that degree.

If I die tonight,

I am the best, you never
heard.

Lick my stomach,
You can taste these hunger
pains.

- One Last Time

I put you on, when I put
these lips on.
Twist those hips and put
these fingertips
To make slow songs.
I put you on from dawn to
dusk--- moonlight and roses.
Bodies rose this--- feeling
with you
When we are closest.

You make me feel like the
woman I want to be.
Every time you exhale and
slip your soul into me.
I swear there's a riverbed
Covered in orange and red
petals,
Where love and death become
one.

My lips are gentle,
My rose tips plant a seed
Just to see you breathe
Rise and fall.
I rise then give you my all

Until I have become the
rainfall
And my eyes are the trees,
The roots are my knees.
The trauma repeats, as our
Spirits dance above the
sheets.
Your teeth release me.

I think this is beyond our
atmosphere,
But no one believes me.
Rowing your poisons through
my hair---
Following my every move
As peaches become bare.

I put you on, while you peal
off my skin
And let the boy in me live
without sin
I become who I always wanted
to be
No more acid, just you and
me.

From your neck to your
navel---
Push, push and I'm able.

Caressing your cheekbones,
rubbing until
There's no more skin tones.

If this isn't paradise,
You are the broth in my soup
and rice
Voodoo love, I can taste the
spells
Seeping from your ribs.

Is it possible you can burn
like ice?
Rawness of love

I am a soldier battling your
thighs
You inhale and whisper--- no
commitments
If someone cums on you,
They just as well may be my
rival.

Only to bring pain--- you
say this way,
This way---
But don't I put you on,
From day to dawn?

You are the sweetest taboo

The ashes from the fire
Whistle against your
collarbone
Just to teach me
That we are both flesh and
bone

Hoping that you respect my
efforts,
How I swam and ran through
deserts
Just so my angry sword
Didn't turn against my queen
of hearts

As I lay you here,
Kissing away our fear,
Hoping that earthquakes
aren't near
That your mind is just here

I put you on,
Turning ordinary
To extraordinary songs.

(October 5, 2015)

- Tarred And Feathered

I asked what I could do
The first time they laughed
and walked away.

The second time I was left
broken
At the bottom of a gutter
With chipped CDs and unkempt
feathers
And the third, there will be
no third time.

I asked what I could do
I poured all my love
From my whispers to my hands
and my shoes
Into the heart shaped box in
front of you.

I asked what I could do,
I stopped asking because
they took that too.
I asked myself what I could
do
And the mirror responded
Love yourself more than they
loved you.

I asked myself, I asked
myself
Until my lips ran out of
fuel
My body tumbled
And my lungs withdrew

I asked him, I asked her
what I could do
As I clinched to tile
And that unpleasant title
stuck like glue.

It tasted like figs and
bitters
Something I outgrew
Five years past due,
An eviction letter,
And mildew

The erosion ate at these
walls
I built for you, I was frail
So I picked up the wax
Letting her and you feather
me too

I asked what I could do
I asked what I could do

Until black tar covered my
lips

I asked him what I could do
Until I couldn't breathe
anymore
I was only breathing you

I asked what I could do
Until I couldn't see myself
anymore

I was just a blur, I asked
what you would do
And now we don't speak
anymore.

I must have forgot
You have become an idea
Buried under a rose plot.

Remembering you passed,
Is as agonizing as my seared
flesh

Now you're just a chisel and
a tombstone

Just remember the trail of
tears

And all that unknown you
feared,

Now it's unknown, but
we're---

Transparent.

- Unknown

Cut me open

I can't do this

Cut me open

I can't be this

What do they want

Tell me

Please God

I don't know who I'm
supposed to be

They want to be free

I just want to find me

Heaven heights,

   3, 4, 5 pills

      To kill to put to sleep

         The memories, the dreams eat at me

         There is no rest place

            Each day serves less faith.

You are going to regret

Something this pure

This lost

This found.

It's 2 A.M., she has 13
    missed calls

- She says I am the one

I am falling apart with each
step,

My eyes are bloodshot

I won't look into the mirror
I fear,

I will never be that girl
again.

- You Tell Me Not To Cry

She swallows me whole,
Yet says I'm a little girl.

I search for my mother in
your arms
Hoping she will approve.

When you both are loving and
cold,
From moment to moment
I walk on eggshells.

If my mother only knew
You are her karma

As I cry in her arms.

(October 27, 2015)

- Unwanted

I was an unwanted seed,

Abortion heavy---
My mama proceeded

To carry me
Away from a cheating man

I found both of them,
In your disdain

- Dear Boy

Surfacing in and out of
consciousness
Blackness, darkness, lights,
. and my fists
Rolling over, my back hit
closure

Rewind, slow motion, too
many drinks

Moving from bars to streets,
to Ubers,
And sheets
Waking up to whiteness,
blood on my thighs,
Soreness and hurt

There he was
Picking peaches from a
forbidden tree
Spreading my chest, like
there was nothing left
Spreading my legs, like a
blank page

In a notebook,
Rewriting who I thought I
was

I remember bits and pieces
My sweats falling off,
Speechless

As if I could reach for God
Pass the clouds, caress his
fingers
And be saved

Rolling over, but I couldn't
Closing my eyes
Numbness inside
Closing my eyes
As tears kiss my lips

There was a soft river
Caught between my teeth

To the boy that took the
part of me
That I thought I could only
give to a woman
A woman that I loved

My body,
My innocence

Now there is just blood and
soreness
An unborn, a fetus, of the
baby her

And I could never have---
So quickly a man can take
The only thing I had

He like the other men
Were going to force me
Peeling back my hands and
knees
To demonstrate that I do
love men

And not the woman stuck to
my side
My eyes, my heart, my
screams
Silently, silently

Replaying every moment,
For a moment, I blamed
myself
Society has made women look
at themselves
Before another

Always questioning ourselves

Three days earlier I left my
lover
To grow, to heal
And you ripped me open
But I won't go under

I keep going

Salt kisses my lips---
trying to conceal
Two losses in one week
I can't take these toxins
anymore.

Closing my eyes,
Hoping it would be over
I cried, as you pulled me
closer

Patriarchy has conquered me
Forcing itself on me---
Forcing itself on me always
In comments--- in
questioning my sexuality

In disrespecting every
woman,
When all I ever wanted was
to love a woman
I was ashamed I didn't tell
anyone,
But I smile and I laugh

Have to pick myself up
Won't let anyone destroy me
Won't let anyone bring me
down

To the boy who thought he
took all of me,
You didn't and I forgive
you.

## DECEMBER, 2015

There are leftover dreams

On my pillowcase

Embers sober me up, you
broke my heart

Didn't you know, didn't you
know.

There are cigarette marks,

Yet no trace, of our love.

- I will never write again

GROWING        PAINS

- Spring

And so it came running,
Like a pair of scissors
A redheaded girl was hunting
The invisible roots I never
knew took hold

I tried to pull the soil
I sowed a patch to the sky
Pulling on the blanket
Trying to shake out the
stars
New flowers began to blossom
Taking root in the cracks in
the concrete
Tasting the citrus stem in
my throat
And the leaves in my palms

There was a new girl with
cherry blossom lips
Who dug a hole for the one
who held onto my wrist
This all took hold
As my blurry vision seeped
away
Silently, so silently
Placing her arms around my
ribs
Until feelings were
unmissable

And she walked into the sun
Only to show me that spring
had come

As I opened my eyes,
The delicate hum turned to a
crackling howl
It must have been the
crackle in her voice
That made nightfall
And there she was standing
tall
With all my thoughts on her
raw fingertips
And all my notes
Folded like a bunch of roses
in her jacket pocket.

That was Spring, Summer, and
Fall
Somehow, and somehow I still
gave it my all.

- Another Girl

Never needed anyone,
That's true sh**
Watch me fly through it
With a full clip
Spit, spit
That's something only real
eyes have seen
No purples, no pinks, no
greens
I've been through pain
That no liquor, drugs, could
clean
Don't want another Ice Queen

You made it clear--- I made
it here
Building up with pure sheer
Loose leaf, verbs, nouns
Though you threw some
adjectives,
Chains, some objective
sayings
You'll remember me.

Not all women are the same,
Not women who held dirt
Can be crowned the same.
This is a high none can
explain

Voodoo love, meditate, heavy
hate
And it weighs on my chest
Give or take.

Reckless girl, I could be as
reckless as you
But I have more to lose
I tasted love once,
And was forced to throw it
all up
Only to wake up with a man's
blood,
Stained all over my thighs
I still keep my chin pressed
to the sky.

They
Come back eventually
Searching for a piece of me
In some pussy, some eyes,
You'll search for a body
As you're touching on their
bodies
You'll search and search
To find nobody

Who really cares

Always,
Feening for plastic, money,
and fear

Women with no assets
Will never take you,

Never remain faithful
When you breakdown
Realize who's really around

Ask God for some faith,
Some sound
He will point to the women
You didn't keep--- bound.

### MAY 2, 2016

Warm whispers, lullabies,
Careless whispers
Trying to write for you,
Even if I'm not, right for
you
Write to show you,
Get to know you.

Close--- that our skin has
become one
Infused, mind misused
Logic blocks the flow.
Manifesting, below,
Further, further into
darkness.
Fruition, a strange fruit
I bit into

I see her hanging onto the
branches
Ignorance and hurt
There is no color here,
Technicolor, so they fear---
The triple minority
She was a young Sade
Soldier for love
Traveling from protest to
protest
And I knew she could not
stay
She was a young Sade

Black curly hair, freckled
face
Moving from place to place
Rounding up our future
And casting it away

Admiring her, I knew
She needed to heal more
women.
Taking the knife to the
ceiling,
She cut the wounds,
Spitting powerful words to
crowds,
To the leaders,
To the healers.

She was my young Sade
Killing me softly,
As she analyzed each and
every line

Saying my work was to pass
time,
Suppressing the looks she
slipped to me
She said I could never get
too close,
Too close to a soldier.

- Letters to God

You were taught to be kind
and beautiful

The roses have bruises, they
shouldn't

Spit, you shouldn't
demonstrate

Colonized body, we're
healing slow.

My brown is lighter so they
wouldn't know

Liquor slow, they want
licking low

But no emotions as the
violence chose

Three, four letters to God.

- For My Friend Mary

Demons come to you,
As they come to me
You hold onto a stem
Though the flower has already
perished
You can hold her once again
But there have been
different bodies on her skin
And the love in others' flesh
Remind you both of this
death

We hold onto the past
Flipping the hourglass,
flipping our glass
Playing tug-of-war with
napkin thoughts
Radio silence,
Pushing her aside, but
pulling women
Who match her image.
It's a sobering emotion
Crawling over our bodies
Only to waterboard us with
hope.
Secretly hoping that one day
She'll call
A few years and we'll live
out those dreams

Another part of us, peels
off our scabs
Knowing they inflicted these
wounds
Knowing we deserve moist
soil
And lemon scented sunlight

We deserve more than an
artificially colored stem

There is only one seed that
needs to grow
That is the world in you.

Paint it and see the demons
drift away
Because there is a world
chipping away at your bones
Screaming to be free,
Shouting for the key
To be the most authentic you
And only with freedom,
Can you be---
Something more than a stem
or sickened memory...

<u>JUNE 18, 2016</u>

Made a collage out of my
favorite silence,

Maybe that's why there's no
response

Because she loves mine,

As much as I loved hers.

- She Is Me

My skins rips, I'm her
Growing, but I'm her
Blue, but I'm her
Running, but I'm her
No she's me.
No they're we
No, no one person
We are all he and she.
Mentally breaking down
Hitting the pavement,
Scrapes and bruises
No lost time just dividing
fuses
I gave my love away,
Discovering unrequited love
was in the way
To being my true self,
Everyday.
She gave her flower away---
But we were already
deceased.

<u>JULY 5, 2016</u>

Growing, growing
My skin breaks, she still
aches
But--- we have one woman
And two different takes.

I give, she takes,
She gives, I take
She gives to her and she and
she
Her to me--- hurts me
We hit then leave
Marks on our bellies
It doesn't make sense,
We are senseless--- can't
sense realness
Not to feel since.

Mistakes never happen
So I misplace memories,
Like they never happened.

I loved her so, I wrote
notes on napkins
Where are you? How did this
occur?
Inspiration, can you find it?

Recalling naps were the
closest to a casket

Roses wrapped around it and
my bed
And all the things she said
Words cannot describe.

So I look for eye rubs,
quick fucks
That's their, not my love.
She's there, but not my
love.

Love, love I let it go,
Like a child's hand
From a man she didn't know
Like a father who didn't
show

I look at both angles, but I
still don't know
The truth.
Maybe I don't want the
answers to all of these
questions,
That way you will always be
sacred and never be tainted.

- Broken Skin

I would like to believe our
euphoric moments
Weren't cultivated from
deception

My heart says no, my mind
says yes.

These stretch marks feel
better,
This broken skin can grow
again---
We grow again, we go again.

Like a seed I was here in
unturned soil
Yet I grew without any
sunlight
They said I would never
reach the moonlight
And they were right, I was
meant to go beyond
What is wrong and right

Only to find myself
somewhere--- language
doesn't exist
I understand that the higher
me, can't dance on this land

They'll realize when they
can't find real eyes
Only starving for depth,
substance--- they slept.

I have been born once again,
barefoot on pavement
Tough, I have been saved
since.

Now there is just emptiness
to rock her to sleep,
They'll fall into theirs, as
the sadness seeps
Into each glare she passes
to me.

I never asked to eat, I just
wrote
More and more poetry.

- You Tell Me I Am Deep

You tell me I am deep,

So deep like a glitch stuck
In between nothingness

Go deeper
Below the surface it's a
curse to feel this
Most people don't know what
they are looking for

Always searching without
knowing
Always touching without
feeling
Always speaking not knowing
the meaning.

You tell me I am deep, go
deeper.
I want to taste the minerals
in your oil
I want to understand your
perception of loyal.

Although speaking isn't
feeling
Although listening isn't
loving

Until there is silence, it's
an unmastered art

It's where something stops
and higher messages start.
It's universal, but most
people don't know
How to use it

You can search and search
You don't know what love is

Until your lips have touched
vulnerability

You have not truly been
heard, until you have
Been face to face with me.

You tell me I am deep,

Will you please elaborate.


(First Date)

# REFLECTION

## AUGUST 7, 2016

She was never truly
cherished until me
And I was never heard by
anybody
It was solitude,
To fall in love,
We should never fall into
anything,
That is pure
Only depression and
insecurities
Make uncertainty a cure

We shouldn't be falling
That isn't love
We are taught to idolize
Emotions that are held
Inside---
But still I rise.

We shouldn't be falling---
in love
But rising to love.
And she rose, and I rose
Separately,
Now her hair on my pillow
Doesn't bother me
Knowing she wanted me to
fall into
Her darkness,

It tried to swallow me
Now I rise to the only woman
calling me,
Myself.

She loves the pretty
lipstick scars on my lips
She loves the music
Dancing in her heart
She loves the sparks
trickling off my tongue
She says my skin is like
honey and milk
She can't fall, she can only
rise
Because love makes watery
eyes
And what is unspoken truly
makes you rise not fall

So baby, know---
That I--- am whole,
Without you.

## AUGUST, 2016

I found courage in blood,

Found courage in love

Poetic tensions, poetic
mentions

The beauty in the shame

The bones to my body frame

Imagine this strange fruit

This is more, this is more

When my lungs hit the air

It is art

They love it when I pour my
heart out

Because you are me, you hear
me, and I feel you

Every energy keeps me true

All of my love for all of
you

We are one so I continue to
perform.

- Reflections

This isn't alcohol
It's rape,
You forced my hips
Molded the shape
Like a man would
Like a boy could
I don't cry too much because
I'm a boy
I cry too much because I'm a
girl

- For Her

I sit down and take out a
pen,

I only want to stroke love
onto your pages and nothing
more

Although, I love to write
for women

Even though they never write
for me

I write and write

Seducing, every ounce

Of your spirit and body.

I am choking on riverbeds
        Can you hear me?
                        - 4 A.M.

- Tensions

If I kept writing could I
get through to you?

You are with her, it
scatters our lucid dreams

So who will take
care of me---
And who can keep up
steadily---
Who has the mental capacity

To divide and sell then come
back to we
And who has already seen---
me?

Just write it down, just
keep quite now
These are building blocks,
The higher I get there is no
stops,
Just mental roadblocks.

In dimensions, other
dimensions
I am sending a sentence, she
is sending a period
I was taking you, they were
never taking me serious.

117

                    Until I took too few, but
                            too many
                      To achieve a higher
                            convention
                    That's how my skin breathes,
                          Poetic lessons.

<u>SEPTEMBER 9, 2016</u>

When was the last time a
woman actually pleased me?

I need love to clear my
mistakes
Three, four,
Love more and more
These women want more back,
They concentrate on more of
what I lack.
I just want art.

You were like contaminated
air,

I needed you, but didn't
know the damage you were
doing

Until it was too late.

## SEPTEMBER 11, 2016

Her skin was like WWII
It survived the brutal war
of men.

- Dreams

You leave me in day,
You leave me at night,
Even in my dreams
It is another woman you grip
tight...

- Quiet Girls

For the girls who want to be
truthful,
But have been told to be
quiet
Quiet down your dresses,
quiet down your lips,
Quiet down the way you roll
your hips.

Her love came in silence
Her music fell off her
eyelids like bits of
polluted rain
Clear, but foggy like a
misty California day.

You were like mud on my new
shoes, exciting yet worn out
Every word that came pouring
out,
Felt like children's kicks
to my ribs,
The more you touched her the
louder the cracks got
You kicked and kicked and
kicked
And when they told me, her
name became the moment
before the vomit

On the floor the rain touched
my cheeks,
My saliva danced in the dirt
I tasted God's mud pies
inside my nose
I stood up and left
But finger sized chips of
other women surfaced with
each bite

The more you moved away from
yourself,
The more you became the bits
of hair I couldn't remove
from my throat
We became the unauthentic
Mexican food I could no
longer stomach

So I wrote,
Until my soft fingers hit the
letters,
Like her father hit her
mother,
They were covered with
blisters and open wounds
Like the childhood I
wouldn't consume
Now only unrealistic words
bleed into my paper
It was a paper cut,

Until blue and purple
bruises soaked my skin,
My body became the diary of
their past.

I learned to drown out the
sound of your lips,
Diluting your cranberry
juice
It was always too sweet for
a soulful woman,

Who only speaks
vulnerability.

To the women,
Who remain as truthful as
the full moon
To the women,
Who count the sounds of
thunder to always remain
loyal
To a sensitive woman,
Who only responded to a
messy world

We have stood up and
survived the men and women
Who have forced hatred onto
our brown and black thighs.

Love      is      greater      than
perceptions   and   ideologies,

Love is burning in stillness.

## SEPTEMBER 16, 2016

Each breath seamlessly
became a note.
A note. Word, I wrote.
And again and again and
again, she---
And again and again and
again, we---
Until I recognized my
sound---
The waves drowned out, my
hips were art, my lips were
sparks--- and, and...I-was-
she
The Goddess-Warrior-Queen
From Aztlan, from my
Technicolor dreams.
Across my hand it screams
Your freedom was here in
this cage all along
Cage all along, page all
along.
Chains in these songs,
change was long, lynching,
credit, typo, edit.
I was a photograph in black
and white.
Never wrong never right.
To the disproportions, that
claim what art is and what
it isn't. Know you are art.
Women are art.

- I Am Ready

A woman I dated,
Once said,
No one would read my poetry
Until I was dead
I have died,
Do you think they will read
it now?

# REBIRTH

What are you soul searching
for?

When the light has always
been you...

<u>SEPTEMBER 28, 2016</u>

I want to drown in you and
be reborn,
Until next year,
Until my veins are bursting
in yay---
Mirror image,
Better than the side, better
than the back.
Top is the only place.
Top---effaced---
Top---she chased---
Top---my lace---
Top---till I shot her
dead---
Cop catcher---they said,
It's better spoken not
read---

Topped until they were
bleeding shame.
Shameless.

Strong enough to bypass the
scars,
The ones you picked with
your teeth.
I love tasting her---it's
cheap.

I want to be engulfed in
your notes.
High, high notes.

She screamed. I wrote.
Redemption, I chose.

The death of me, was the
rise of her.
And now there's no knowing
where she'll go.
Up, up, left, left---mic
one---check, check.
Center---stage---left---
page---
Writing---saved---she---
Caged---I---broke---free---
I saved---me.

## SEPTEMBER 28, 2016

I wrote tonight
I want to play with your
black curly hair
And lick your thorns
Until you have picked me up
and let me down.

I dove into the underworld
Like bloody nails and
splitters.
The ones you carved into my
pale skin
I took two steps forward and
eight back.
You were the love of my
life,
Until one drop of her
Cut me deeper than my roots,
Deeper than conquest,
Go deeper than her breast,
Chains and oppressed.

Great Grandmother,
Released smoke and blew in
death
Whiskey and whistle calls
Women, she loved them all

As I plucked a feather, a
Goddess told me
She once said
The lines in my lips

Were a revolution
Made of maize, beauty,
spices, a fusion.

Peppers and love,
Chili was cooked every
weekend by my grandmother
If it was hot she was mad
And if his tongue broke the
Ten Commandments
She would chant a curse.
Drums, mud
Hearts and blood.

I was always told to behave,
Cook and clean
Then be saved.
Be that woman, Virgin Mary
enslaved

And I was, my beloved
I was as faithful as our
Mexican murals
What more could you want?

She told me to be a woman,
I said I'd be a man
Pebbles dropped onto my
grave
And you decorated them
With baseball caps and
another woman.

- Letters From 1521

My love,

What would she say?
I place the image of my
lover
On the left hand of the
other woman.
Carving the heart of my
innocent love,
La Azteca.
So I could eat dinner
And more pussy.
I have made my flame drown
Titanic, she was.
Sorrow,
Like the morning after
conquest

And there she stands,
The love of my life
Church bells ring

It's only the beginning,
Of blood she has shared.
-Your Cortez

Goodbye my beloved
I will not weep
Anything less than
Christianity

And my indigenous roots.

You are free,
I pay one more visit to our
unborn baby
Woman to woman,
Sheet to sheet.
Only on the Day of the Dead
Was I crowned Goddess,
Queen.

From the velvet lips of
other women,
To your ghost
And a boy
I lost my innocence.

This is not poetry.
This is not love.
This is me,

Growing up.
This is the future
She promised me,
Vividly. Emotionally.
Silently.

Like broken bones under
churches,
We all mend
That is not love,
It is growth.

<u>OCTOBER 1, 2016</u>

You are not in love with
them
You are in love with the
potential

You believed they could be,

You took ugliness and
brokenness

And like the artist you are,
You created something
beautiful

Never realizing how radiant
you are,
How capable you are

I see your love it is
vibrant,
I feel your energy I
survived it

That was just an idea, but
you,
You are a fact

You are a child,
Who just happened to react

Moments don't last and
theories

Go way back

They say you are a lot to
handle,
I am ready to help you
unpack

You are phenomenal.

<u>OCTOBER 2, 2016</u>

I woke up buried in flowers
and zinc,
There she was, there I was.
I have seen her before,
I have chased her through
the caves of my heart
Petals stuck to her feet,
Pink fluid bathed her knees.

She never looked back,
She just danced and danced

I was as invisible as a
woman's cry
I was as unspoken as these
dry mornings and sedated
nights
I was tasteless like these
melancholy oceans,
And vivid red lipstick
dreams.

No beauty could save me from
her uninterested tone,
I should smile more, but I
didn't want to.

Pretty little girls, echoed
my name
They weren't her.
They couldn't quench this
cottonmouth

No it stemmed back too many
                 lives,
          I have lost count.

I write every day,
unknowingly.

Speaking to the only God I
know, myself.

- Free Flowing Thoughts


I seep into solitude,
Like the first time I tasted
your thighs

She wants my future,
I crave her past,
I conducted melodies on her
hourglass

You tasted heaven, but
wanted hell

The smell of her evades my
bedroom,
Bruja love potions

Your skin holds oceans of
me,
Some of your girlfriends say

You speak of a woman with a
black rose.

Past life, 1805
- I am awake

Whole generations vanished
after I spoke.

I have kissed enough demons
to condemn this world,
I have screwed enough angels
to question the "girl"
Breathtaking flesh, you are
the Sun
You are the Rain,
everything---
And nothing I wish I could
be
The clay is forming
I have yet to see...
With Mother Earth, what are
we?
I can sow my own wounds,
I have moved through
crescent moons
It must be this shaman
cocoon
That could only be awakened
by tü.
By you, mi amor
How many times must we
reincarnate?

I didn't want to hear it,
But the bags under my eyes
carried
My strengths and weaknesses.

- In Search For Love Again

She was always all of hers
        before mine

And I will always be mine
        before hers.

(October 12, 2016)

I searched through pictures,
I moved through sex,
I met women,
I got undressed.

I am the moon,
I am the sun.
I am growing like everyone.
I was broken like everyone.

I am the seed,
I am death.
I have smelled her perfume
I have known, what she
selects.
I know her neck.
I know the crease
In her chest.

I have been high,
I have been low.
I battled for her,
I have let her go.

I have survived her and I.

How can you be so strong?
Yet so weak.

<u>OCTOBER 21, 2016</u>

There is no ownership in
love
I give all of me to me
She gives all of her to her.

I pick a cherry and place it
between your lips,

I think of you and I know
this

This is happiness,
This is me,
Kissing the corner of your
smile,

These are the reasons I have
lost all track of time
You are timeless,
Gravity isn't here,

I love you,
Despite that you are
neither,
Far nor near

I used to love in fear,
Now I love the woman in the
mirror

I open my eyes,
I have let the image of you
and her die,
Because I have realized
I don't want to love, who we
used to be

I love women who speak in
whole,
I love women who have
learned to let go.

## OCTOBER 26, 2016

He knocks on my lips
Telling me to open
Innocence seeps out of my
mouth
I forgot how to speak.
Silenced by friends,
Cousins,
Students.
They have gone to places
That were never meant for
them.
So when you touch me,
I slip into darkness and
slowly open up.

- For Myself

You don't see the love

Tucked in between the
moments of nothingness

You never had peace before
you were in pieces

Trying to piece together
words that were never yours
Trying to make sense of
actions that were only hers

You don't look at you, you
look at them
You don't accept love, you
just give
You've taught yourself
How to say sorry for them
and how to forgive
Yet you've never forgiven
yourself

Depleted,
You only look for growth,
Never letting the flower
live,
There's value and love
within every moment

There you are, there she is

Writing again and again

Purposely, quietly,
tirelessly for herself.

- Beauty of Solitude

You are becoming the woman,
you always needed as a
child.

<u>NOVEMBER 7, 2016</u>

You can tell me you love me
Then inhale my soul
I can tell you I love you
Then learn to let go.

(For her)

To be one
To be free
To be here (her)
To be me
This is love.

- Still her

White cloth
White candles
Does this mean I'm pure?
Silence echoes off my tongue
There is dry blood on my
thighs
You say this is alcohol,
Moments pass
Maybe years
Maybe 500
My wrists are tied by your
fingers
A sacrifice to your ancestors
It might be the alcohol,
But he doesn't drink much
I think it is rape,
I wish I didn't think
At 3:27 A.M.

- Future Love

Like fractures and unknown
paths
I hear my heart glide,
Touching the sweat of
women's backs
Searching for cues as the
violin guides me
To something new or old,
I can't differentiate the
two

Only in the solitude of
empty midnights
Have I validated the motion
in her eyes
How can I go and where will
we be
But I have written you in
and scratched you out
Story after story
Character after character

I romance the miles between
us
How graceful I am to be
dipped
In passion and loneliness

My heart flutters at the
thought of writing
Of loving

Of listening to my wife
I have loved her before she
even knew
I have captured poems and
the scent of her perfume
No love can die when it's
scattered
In your breath

Embedded in my art
I write only what I feel
I write only what you kill
But I wonder at 9:59 when it
will begin
The moment, I lay eyes on
you,
I dream,
I have dreamt about you.

(Where are you)

THE          RETURN

<u>DECEMBER 4, 2016</u>

I received a message from
you last night,
You resurrected old feelings
that no woman should bare.

(14 months later)

Logically we couldn't speak
This is more than biology
My hands, my knees, my feet
One word, I sweat
My heartbeat
The heat

You miss me,
I taste defeat
She said I know

And it really didn't matter
Because we both knew
We have been here before
For many years, through many
tears
In silence.

- Old Wounds

You tell me you miss me,
My mind goes running like a
motherless child

I waited for this day,
praying
Hoping it would never come.

I thought for sure my
bitterness
Would spoil your taste buds
Convincing your tongue to
try another,
But only love came spilling
out of my chest.

I tried to stop, I plunged,
I fed my mouth with gauze
to quiet the moans and war
cries
But my love for you was too
grand

Even when you left me dying
With feverish anger and
cholera
I thought it was over,
But just one word and I
Wanted to rise like the moon
And die like the sun.

I was out of breath
And she was out of sight
Like a wildfire my heart
begged
To reunite,

Grew,
It crackled with every
message
Releasing ever memory
For that moment I saw our
dreams
Become reborn, and our stars
reinstated
I wondered if I could dig up
our baby
Because if you said yes.
I'd say I do, but I knew
This was nothing more than
taboos

What a fool I would be
To hand my love back to you.

<u>DECEMBER 5, 2016</u>

No one could love you the
way I did
Yet you come, you go
With soothing whispers
Trembling lies
Knowing I've died seven
times
Hoping I lie eight

Feeling love and hate
You only come to measure
your power

You want me to remain
forever loyal
To vicious cycles
You must be here just to
see,
Then leave---
Me hanging.

So who am I to judge
Always forgiving
Remembering we all bleed
We all seek freedom

Are you back to stay
Or do you just hate sleeping
alone?

It is crystalized,
Chances rarely come twice.

All I ever wanted was the
truth,
Regardless they judge me for
seeing you.

## DECEMBER 20, 2016

This isn't for you,
Yet it is written about you.

## DECEMBER 22, 2016

Moon, planets
Move, movement
Change, illusion,
Season, conclusion

I cannot handle it
I am cracked open
Like heartbreak, devolution
It is an evolution
For me to demonstrate my
emotions
Publicly, for you

I have fallen into hidden
childhood wounds
Swimming in a void, I
thought I outgrew

With you, I am raw, naked,
Exposed.

With you, I am careless, yet
truthful,
And loving.

- Left In The Cold

I have cried myself to
sleep,
Pushing my family off of me
Pretending like everything
is okay.
It will be only a little bit
longer,
Before I can no longer
Keep my spirit up.

Lost girl, please learn your
lesson.
This cannot be the end.

(Christmas Day)

<u>DECEMBER 26, 2016</u>


My love,

Do you know who I am?
When your eyes touch mine
Will you awake this time?


I taste life and death
As if we are a cycle
It is rooted in my soul
So when you leave, you come,
you go
I know I have felt this
heartbreak before
I loved you in multiple
lifetimes


Visions
Of my death,
They told me I was going to
take my life
A choice in 2015
We were here to wake each
other up


I woke up,
This is unconditional
You taught me
Karmic, this is beyond us
Spiritual.


I was never enough for you,

You never wanted to commit
to,
I believe this is what was
meant to occur
I think we made this promise
a long time ago,
But my ego wouldn't let me
see us whole.

You were my life and my
death,
But I broke my skin and was
born once again.

- Untitled

You speak as if I am a
little girl,

I became a woman a long time
ago.

## DECEMBER 29, 2016

Only words can save me
Only I can create my future
Only the sky can break me---
up

Only a lie can shake them---
up
Only God knows why,
Head up

I have to say goodbye
Say thank you, releasing
hurricanes
From my sight

I cried and cried
Cause she's not mine
Cause I had to let our dreams
die
For the first time, I know
what it's like to live

The universe said it's time
to give it up.

# DISSOLUTION

EXT. GAY BAR - NIGHT

Intoxicated, Alyssa stands in line with
her hyperactive lesbian friend ROSA
(23). Alyssa's vision is slammed; drunk
men and women are pushing themselves
through the crowd. Left and right.
Alyssa slowly lifts her head. Suddenly
all TIME stops.

We see everything freeze except Alyssa
and Rain. As if she has been hit by a
truck--- frozen--- she can't move. We
hear her heartbeat off in the distance.
They lock eyes. Rain looks away.

Regaining her awareness, Alyssa struts
in her high heels toward her as if she
is on a runway.

Alyssa is so close she can almost kiss
her. She sarcastically asks.

                    ALYSSA
              What's up, how
              are you?

Hesitating, Rain forces herself to look
Alyssa in the eyes.

                    RAIN
            Hi.

Alyssa's confidence seamlessly drifts
away. She is struck with warmness. We
SEE color cover her face for the first
time.

                    ALYSSA
            Where are you going?

                    RAIN
            To this bar.

                    ALYSSA
            Me too.

Rain and Alyssa walk into the line.

Both continue to gaze at each other as
the line rapidly moves.

Rain caresses her hand, holding it as if
time were never an issue.

<u>FEBRUARY 12, 2017</u>

She cries, as I speak of the
sexual assault

We both split open

Releasing the baggage

That was never ours to
carry.

20 going to be 21
You were 22 going to be 23

Now I am 23
And you are 25
Have we changed?

I am only passionate with
you,

I have only made love to
you.

If tonight were my last
night,
I would die happy,
Knowing I got to spend it
with you.

<u>FEBRUARY 14, 2017</u>

I feel you with me,
Everywhere I go
Placing love in my left
pocket
And sowing God in my eyes,
Never letting me run over.

A smile cracks,
You are my earthquakes
And waterfalls
You are the faults I've
learned to love
And the body I've learned to
cherish

You caress this landfill
As you cultivate landscapes
From battle wounds and ashes
Grounding me, pouring water
Between two cups

My alchemist,
You lift me up, up,
As I pick her up, up.
Planting me back in the sky
And every night
I get to see my roots
strengthen.

I love I, and I love you
And though I could never
stay with a woman

I always knew
It's because my soul has yet
to meet you.

I search for you like a
fatherless child,
Through binding roads I've
walked for miles,
Through women's laughs and
crooked smiles.
Loving them like they were
me,
And hoping they were you.

Tired, yet the bond is
always there,
Even when our blistered
soles seem repaired.

I fear I will run from you,

So they can never say you
left me, again.

## MARCH 2, 2017

That must be God speaking
From me to you

Where I end, they begin
That's between us
No secrets run deeper
Like love from your arching
body to my fingertips
Going in and out,
We break barriers and
droughts
Switch positions
Your peach melts into the
palm of my hand
This must be the tree of
life,
That created women.

Us making love drowning out
the ceilings
I put you on my mouth,
I drink what you'd felt,
I feel your body out,
As if it never left me.

Flip you from behind,
Telepathy says you're fine
Old memories collide
As we mix what is yours and
mine,
Angels cry and old systems
fall.

Painting with every touch,
You crumble into my arms,
As dawn finally approaches
us.

- Performing

They can take it all,
Not your soul.
They can take your body,
But still I go, go, go.
When you got soul, soul,
soul
It's difficult to not let
others know
How you grew from ashes to
fire,
Broken to something higher.
Speaking as a reminder
To love past the desire of
fools gold.

If these words sold inner
love,
I would do it again and
again
So you wouldn't have to cry
pressing send
So you'd never have to say
goodbye to any moms,
Dads, close friends.
They can break us down, but
we still mend.
Red Dollars couldn't really
make ends.

I have you like way, way up

As if God sent me down
whenever you got stuck.
Hope you know it's real,
real love
Not Bobby and Whitney
Or your daddy and grandmas,
But J. Dilla and Ghostface
Killah.
Vanilla and French kiss---
Only my 5 year old self can
hold this, type of crush.

If I don't make it,
Know this performance is
sacred
To you and I.

They can kill our spirit,
but still we survive.
I hold you in my heart
That's real, real life.
Look how we can go,
When you give a mic to a
childlike girl.
Doing it all to real life,
To realize how my family
deserves
Really nice things and you
deserve double triple rings.

All those nights I collected
tears and screams,

Know we fit perfect in our
dreams.
We deserve it that's all I
mean
I'll write it all for you
and me.
So the world can see
How beautiful our people
are.
How beautiful I think we
are.

<u>MARCH, 2017</u>

In darkness, you moan

Telling me you are all mine.

<u>MARCH 27, 2017</u>

You wanted roses,
So I rose to a higher me.
If that isn't love,
I don't know what you're
trying to see.
Love letters and roses
They send but they lie and
cheat.
I just give to you
What they cannot taste
Cause it's real
No one can take my space.
I don't have to be up in
your face
For you to know
I cared for you in darkness
Spark this, solar system
You are the sweat on my skin
My first breath after sin
Sunday mornings
Writing again.
Is she mine, is she there
Does she think, does she
dare
To come close?

It's never close enough
I'll eat cereal for the both
of us
Childish, but she knows
we're tough

Like bruises on our parents
That rough, but not that
love.
Loosen that grip,
You just might find
What you've been searching
for
In shot glasses
And morning sunrises.

She tells me I am her
favorite poet,
That's all I ever wanted to
hear.

<u>APRIL 6, 2017</u>

If I could sit here all day,
I would.
Passing time, moments last
Less drama, more romance
Flipping our glass, paint
your hourglass
They wouldn't understand it,
Most can't comprehend what
was given and taken.
Reunited, they think it's
fake.
Fake love, they just take
and take.

If you were to dive
Deep, deep inside
You would find a woman,
Who's just trying to make it

Deep, deep you'd find our
love hid--- sacred
I'd drop to my knees,
If the God in me was
pleased.

Imagine a future without me,
When bits of your past were
left without me.
I cut you with my words
Like little bits of razors

Childhood wounds, yet the
scars are savored.
We were so young, watermelon
flavored

Spinning and spinning,
You have me spinning and
spinning
Can't express half of what I
feel,
When I stare into your
beautiful brown eyes--- it's
still--- there.

Don't run from me,
Just love all of me.
The blood on my thighs,
The kisses, the replies,
The moment, the goodbyes
Only to find you tucked into
my side,
I've learned patience.
Happiness, tears, eyes.

This something can't be
another empty statement
Every comment, I work it
Deep in my stream
Regardless this has to be
more than
Merely, a solo dream

Deep down it seems like I
have it all together,
But what does that even mean
If there are only incomplete
kisses in between
Rose lips,
Would you move on by the
weekend?
Are you awake? Sleeping?
If I wrote, would you sing
If I said it, would you know
what I meant?

Pockets full of secrets,
Baby would you seek it
Time doesn't exist near you,
Time only times me to be
clear,
Of us here, fear no touch---
No fuck, no lust,
Just bodies, spirit, us.

- Late Night Thoughts

Pieces of me go missing
Like rubber bands--- I never
know where or how.
Until I meet the women
You claimed were whole.

Adjectives. Nouns. Verbs.
Have you gotten your point
across?

If love was never what you
wanted,

I was never an artist...

- When You Don't Reply

This is the third time,
I meant to shove emptiness
in your ear
Instead the innocence in me
Brought you to my bed, where
it all began.
Why must you only love
the past, when I am the
present...
You crave me, like a last
response.

Trying to build each other
up, with legs spread
There wouldn't be a fourth
Emptiness, innocence
They all have
What was never mine.

You only cry, when no one
hears...

I am exhausted and tongue-
tied with goodbyes.

You tumbled into my arms
Cheated. Choked. Abused.
I nurtured you
Kissing your forehead,
As you slept
Now your body language says,
You want to be free.

(April 2017)

She is withdrawing again,
You say you like me,
Yet you have all this
baggage

You said she was nothing,
Now you say she is something

And I could never fill that
space

My soul cries,
As you stare at me blankly.

You are deserving,
Of the highest form of love.
Life is the highs, lows,
And in-betweens.

- Insomniac

I am a zombie
The prelude to an ending

Tunneled dreams, buried
corps,
Fire, dust

Kaleidoscope

The moon highlights your
tattoos
You are in a deep slumber

The pulse of the night taps
Into my infatuation,
Of a woman,
I don't even know.

(A.C.)

- Evolution

Evolutions are embedded in
these skins,
I trace your spine
As if you are the book
I never wrote.

- Sadness

You haunt me,

So I squeeze my eyes shut

Like my younger self.

There is distance,

Even though she is inside of
me

All that's lost,

All at the cost of
indecision.

She is always willing to
spread her legs
Like peanut butter on wheat
bread

She wants you to eat, suck
fingers, and seeds,
Making you believe

You are her last dinner
date.

Battered, abused
My heart still thrives.

What a privilege it is,
To sample true love
Pass, chew, and spit it out
At your convenience.

<u>APRIL, 2017</u>

Filling cups of my hands,
With water,
Two, three.

I am pouring,
Rubbing my body with roses.
It's become a ritual to love
myself.

I wipe her off my skin,
You are no more than a
distant friend.

She is deceased
And I now see this woman
clearly.

- Hurricane

I am a hurricane and a sunny
day
Thunderstorms,
I regain consciousness
Picking myself up
Loving the strengths and the
weaknesses
In the grooves in my back,
Loving the beauty and
madness in my lap
If you can't appreciate the
storm
Leave before my sun
oversteps its boundaries.

You never thought this day
would come,
Neither did I.
You had me wrapped around
your thumb,
Spinning like an endless
ball of yarn---

Freedom.
I tear these strings,
There is no more fear.

Loneliness:

Comes when we are furthest
from ourselves.

Sad children, make strong
women.

APRIL 23, 2017

Acceptance,
Is learning the woman you
love,
Was never yours to love.

I can never find the correct
words to say,
Moment, after moment...
After moment...

I don't want you to go,
But I know I cannot stay
With mouths shut

My pride wins again.

- My love

I apologize

For all I have done

I am no saint,

Nor am I a sinner.

After two years
I am okay with writing
These pages for you and
tossing
Them out
Regardless,
If you read this or not.

You
    Will
        Never
            Forget
                Me

And
    I
Forgive
    You.

<u>MAY 2017</u>

I close this book,

Knowing there is another

Waiting to be written.

- For The Reader

If you are reading this,
We are still alive.

<u>MAY 2017</u>

THE END

Made in the USA
San Bernardino, CA
23 April 2018